# Basics of ChatGPT

## Will Atkins

# Table of Contents

# Part I: Introduction

## Chapter 1. Getting to Know ChatGPT

In recent years, there has been significant progress in the field of Natural Language Processing (NLP), and ChatGPT is one of the most important developments in this area. The model has received a lot of attention due to its ability to generate natural language responses that are both coherent and relevant, making it a valuable tool for a wide range of applications.

ChatGPT is a type of machine learning model that uses artificial intelligence (AI) to generate natural language responses to user input. It is a neural network-based model that has been trained on large datasets of human language to develop a deep understanding of language patterns and structures. The model uses a transformer architecture, which was introduced in 2017 by researchers at Google, to process sequential data such as text or speech.

The transformer architecture was a significant advancement in the field of NLP because it allowed for the training of deep neural networks that could process sequences of variable length. This was a departure from previous approaches that relied on hand-engineered features and shallow models, which were often limited in their ability to capture the complexity of natural language. The transformer architecture enabled the development of much more sophisticated models that could learn directly from large amounts of data, without the need for hand-engineering.

ChatGPT is a specific type of transformer model that has been pre-trained on a massive amount of text data. The model has been trained on billions of tokens of text data from the internet, which has given it a deep understanding of language patterns and structures. The pre-training process involves training the model on a task called language modeling, where the model is trained to predict the next word in a sentence given the previous words. This process allows the model to learn the statistical regularities of natural language, such as word co-occurrences and syntactic structures.

Once the model has been pre-trained, it can be fine-tuned on a specific task, such as question answering, dialogue generation, or text completion. Fine-tuning involves training the model on a smaller dataset of examples specific to the task at hand, which allows the model to adapt to the specific characteristics of the task.

One of the key benefits of ChatGPT is its ability to generate responses that are tailored to the specific context of a conversation. This means that it is able to understand the nuances of language and generate responses that are appropriate for the specific conversation it is having. For example, if a user is asking about a specific product, ChatGPT is able to understand the context of the conversation and provide relevant information about the product in question. Similarly, if a user is expressing an emotion, ChatGPT can recognize the sentiment and generate a response that is appropriate for that emotion.

Another important benefit of ChatGPT is its ability to learn from user input. When a user interacts with ChatGPT, the model is able to learn from the conversation and adapt its responses accordingly. This means that over time, ChatGPT becomes more intelligent and better equipped to handle a wide range of user interactions. For example, if a user consistently asks about a particular topic, ChatGPT will learn to prioritize that topic and generate more accurate and relevant responses related to it.

Overall, the introduction of ChatGPT has been a significant development in the field of NLP. The model's ability to generate natural language responses that are both coherent and relevant makes it a powerful tool for a wide range of applications, such as customer service, education, and creative writing. As we continue to explore the capabilities of ChatGPT, we can expect to see even more innovative applications of this technology in the future.

One area where ChatGPT has shown great promise is in the field of conversational agents or chatbots. Chatbots are computer programs designed to simulate human conversation, and they are used in a wide range of applications, such as customer service, virtual assistants, and language learning. However, traditional chatbots often suffer from a lack of coherence and relevance in their responses, which can lead to frustration and a poor user experience.

ChatGPT has the potential to address many of these issues by providing a more intelligent and adaptable conversational agent. By using a pre-trained model and fine-tuning it on specific tasks, ChatGPT can generate more relevant and coherent responses to user input. Moreover, its ability to learn from user interactions over time means that it can become even more intelligent and accurate in its responses.

Another area where ChatGPT has shown great promise is in the field of creative writing. In recent years, there has been an increasing interest in using AI to generate creative content, such as poetry, fiction, and music. ChatGPT's ability to generate natural language responses makes it a valuable tool for creative writing, as it can provide inspiration and generate new ideas based on user input.

For example, ChatGPT has been used to generate new dialogue for TV shows and movies, as well as to assist with creative writing tasks such as generating plot outlines and character descriptions. While ChatGPT is not yet able to replace human creativity, it has the potential to augment and enhance the creative process, making it a valuable tool for writers and other creative professionals.

In the chapters that follow, we will dive deeper into these topics, explaining how ChatGPT works and how you can interact, understand, and customize ChatGPT to your needs; provide examples of ChatGPT in use in customer service, education, and creative writing; and provide ethical considerations, limitations and challenges, and illustrate some of ChatGPT's future potential.

# Chapter 2. How ChatGPT Works

At its core, ChatGPT is a type of neural network called a transformer model. The transformer architecture was introduced in 2017 by Google researchers, and it quickly became a key component of many state-of-the-art natural language processing models. The transformer architecture is based on the idea of self-attention, which allows the model to focus on specific parts of the input sequence when generating its output.

The transformer is made up of multiple layers, and each layer has two parts: a multi-head attention mechanism and a feedforward neural network. In simple terms, the multi-head attention mechanism allows the transformer to focus on different parts of the input text at the same time, which is important for understanding the context and meaning of the text. The feedforward neural network processes the output from the multi-head attention mechanism to generate the final output. Overall, this transformer architecture is an important part of ChatGPT that allows it to understand and generate natural language responses. For those that struggled to keep up with this paragraph, feel free to skip to the next section, but if you're a glutton for punishment, we provide more details on this process below.

During the training process, the transformer network processes an input sequence in a series of layers, with each layer transforming the input representation into a higher-level abstraction. The input to each layer is a sequence of vectors, where each vector corresponds to a token or word in the input sequence. The output of each layer is another sequence of vectors, which is passed to the next layer in the network.

The multi-head attention mechanism is a key component of each layer. It computes a weighted sum of the input vectors, where the weights are determined by an attention distribution. The attention distribution is computed by comparing each input vector to all the other input vectors using a similarity function. The result is a set of attention scores, which are used to weight the input vectors in the weighted sum.

The feedforward neural network applies two linear transformations followed by a non-linear activation function to the output of the attention mechanism. The first transformation projects the output of the attention mechanism to a higher-dimensional space, while the second transformation projects it back to the original dimensionality. The non-linear activation function introduces non-linearities into the network, allowing it to learn complex representations of the input sequence.

Overall, the transformer architecture is a powerful and flexible neural network architecture that has achieved state-of-the-art results on a wide range of NLP tasks. Its multi-head attention mechanism and feedforward neural network layers enable it to effectively model the relationships between words and generate high-quality text.

## Pre-Training

ChatGPT uses a specific variant of the transformer architecture called GPT, or Generative Pre-training Transformer. GPT is a large-scale language model that has been trained on a massive corpus of text data, such as books, articles, and web pages. The pre-training process involves training the model on a large amount of text data using a language modeling task, where the model is trained to predict the next word in a sequence given the previous words.

This pre-training process allows the model to learn a general understanding of natural language, including syntax, semantics, and pragmatics. Once the model has been pre-trained, it can be fine-tuned on specific tasks, such as language translation or sentiment analysis. Fine-tuning involves training the model on a smaller dataset of task-specific examples, allowing it to learn to generate more relevant and accurate responses for that task.

One of the key features of ChatGPT is its ability to generate coherent and relevant responses to user input. This is achieved through the use of a decoding algorithm called beam search, which generates a set of candidate responses and selects the most likely one based on a scoring function. The scoring function takes into account factors such as the coherence and relevance of the response, as well as the diversity of the generated responses.

Another important feature of ChatGPT is its ability to learn from user interactions over time. This is achieved through the use of a technique called reinforcement learning, where the model is rewarded for generating responses that are rated positively by users. By continually learning from user interactions, the model can become even more intelligent and accurate in its responses over time.

While ChatGPT is an impressive natural language processing model, it is not without its limitations. One major challenge with ChatGPT and other large-scale language models is their high computational and memory requirements. Training and deploying these models requires significant computing resources, which can make them inaccessible for many researchers and developers. Additionally, there are concerns around the ethical and societal implications of using AI to generate natural language, such as the potential for bias and the risk of malicious use.

Another limitation of ChatGPT is its inability to understand context in the same way that humans do. While the model can generate responses that are coherent and relevant based on the input it receives, it does not have a deep understanding of the underlying meaning or context of the conversation. This can lead to responses that are technically correct but may miss the intended meaning or fail to take into account important details.

Additionally, ChatGPT has been shown to have biases that reflect the biases present in the training data. For example, a study by researchers at Stanford University found that the model generated biased language related to race and gender, with responses that reflected and reinforced stereotypical views and attitudes. Addressing these biases and ensuring that natural language processing models are trained on diverse and representative datasets is a crucial area of research for the field.

One way that researchers are working to address the limitations of ChatGPT and other natural language processing models is through the development of hybrid models that combine the strengths of multiple models. For example, some researchers have explored the use of a hybrid model that combines ChatGPT with a symbolic reasoning system to improve the model's ability to understand context and generate more accurate responses.

Another promising area of research for natural language processing is the development of models that can generate explanations for their decisions and responses. This is an important area of research for ensuring the transparency and accountability of AI models, particularly in applications such as healthcare and legal decision-making where the stakes are high.

Despite its limitations, ChatGPT and other large-scale language models represent a significant advance in the field of natural language processing, and have the potential to revolutionize the way we interact with technology. From virtual assistants and chatbots to automated language translation and content generation, natural language processing models like ChatGPT are already having a significant impact on a wide range of industries and applications.

As the field continues to evolve, it is essential that researchers and developers prioritize the ethical and societal implications of their work, and work to ensure that these powerful technologies are used in ways that are fair, transparent, and beneficial for all. With careful consideration and responsible development, natural language processing models like ChatGPT have the potential to transform the way we communicate, learn, and interact with the world around us.

# Part II: Using ChatGPT

## Chapter 3. Interacting with ChatGPT

In addition to the practical applications of natural language processing discussed earlier, this technology is also being used in a wide range of research fields. For example, natural language processing is being used in the field of linguistics to explore the fundamental properties of language and the ways in which it is structured and processed in the brain.

One of the key challenges in linguistics is understanding the relationship between language and meaning. Natural language processing has been used to create computational models of meaning that can help researchers better understand how meaning is represented and processed in the brain.

These models are based on large-scale language models like ChatGPT and are trained on vast amounts of text data to identify patterns and associations between words and concepts. By analyzing these patterns and associations, researchers can gain insights into the structure of meaning and the ways in which it is processed in the brain.

In addition to linguistics, natural language processing is also being used in the field of psychology to explore the ways in which language is used to express emotions and convey social information. For example, researchers are using natural language processing to analyze social media data and identify patterns in the ways in which people use language to express emotions like happiness, sadness, and anger.

By analyzing these patterns, researchers can gain insights into the emotional states of individuals and groups and the factors that contribute to emotional expression. This research has implications for a wide range of fields, from mental health to social media marketing.

Another area where natural language processing is having a significant impact is in the field of education. Researchers are using natural language processing to develop intelligent tutoring systems that can provide personalized feedback and assistance to students. For example, an intelligent tutoring system may analyze a student's writing and provide feedback on grammar, syntax, and style. By providing personalized feedback and guidance, these systems can help students improve their writing skills and achieve better academic outcomes. In addition to providing feedback, intelligent tutoring systems can also adapt to the individual learning styles and preferences of each student. By analyzing a student's performance and learning patterns, these systems can adjust their instruction and provide personalized recommendations for additional learning resources and activities.

Natural language processing is also being used to develop educational chatbots that can provide students with on-demand assistance and support. These chatbots can answer questions, provide feedback, and offer personalized recommendations based on the student's performance and learning history.

In the field of healthcare, natural language processing is being used to improve the accuracy and efficiency of clinical documentation. Doctors and other healthcare professionals can use natural language processing software to transcribe their notes and other documentation, reducing the risk of errors and improving the speed and accuracy of the process. In addition to clinical documentation, natural language processing is also being used to develop virtual health assistants that can provide patients with personalized health advice and support. These assistants can analyze a patient's symptoms and medical history and provide recommendations for treatment, medication, and other healthcare interventions.

Natural language processing is also being used to analyze large datasets in the field of social science. For example, researchers are using natural language processing to analyze social media data and identify patterns in the ways in which people communicate and interact online. By analyzing these patterns, researchers can gain insights into social and cultural phenomena, such as the spread of misinformation and the formation of online communities. This research has implications for a wide range of fields, from politics to marketing.

Despite the many exciting applications of natural language processing, there are also significant challenges and ethical considerations that must be addressed. One of the most pressing concerns is the potential for natural language processing to perpetuate or amplify biases and stereotypes. For example, language models trained on biased datasets may produce responses that reflect and reinforce stereotypes related to race, gender, or other demographic factors. This can have serious implications for individuals and society as a whole, perpetuating discrimination and exacerbating existing inequalities.

To address these concerns, researchers and practitioners in the field of natural language processing are working to develop more inclusive and diverse datasets and to create models that are less susceptible to bias. This requires a deep understanding of the social and cultural context in which language is used, as well as a commitment to ethical practices and principles.

Another challenge in the field of natural language processing is the difficulty of understanding and interpreting the results generated by these models. Language is a complex and multifaceted phenomenon, and even the most advanced language models are limited in their ability to capture its full richness and nuance. As a result, it is important for researchers and practitioners to exercise caution and humility when working with natural language processing technologies. This means acknowledging their limitations and using them in conjunction with other methods and tools to gain a more comprehensive understanding of language and its role in human communication and cognition.

In conclusion, natural language processing is a rapidly evolving field with a wide range of practical applications in industry, research, and education. It holds the potential to revolutionize the way we communicate and interact with technology, and to provide new insights into the structure and processing of language in the human brain.

As the field of natural language processing continues to evolve and grow, it will be important for scholars and researchers to stay up-to-date on the latest developments and to engage in ongoing discussions and debates about the ethical, social, and cultural implications of these technologies.

# Chapter 4. Understanding ChatGPT Responses

In this chapter, we'll focus on examining and analyzing the responses generated by GPT-based chatbots, with the goal of improving their quality and accuracy. We will discuss the key challenges in generating high-quality responses, explore different approaches to evaluating response quality, and examine strategies for improving the performance of GPT-based chatbots.

Understanding ChatGPT responses is an essential aspect of building effective chatbots and natural language processing (NLP) applications. ChatGPT is designed to generate text responses that are coherent and contextually relevant, but it is not always easy to predict or control the specific responses that the model will generate. Therefore, it is important to have a solid understanding of how ChatGPT works and how it generates its responses.

To understand how ChatGPT generates responses, it is useful to examine some examples. Suppose we prompt ChatGPT with the following statement: "What is your favorite color?" The model may generate a response like "I don't have eyes, so I don't have a favorite color." This response demonstrates the ability of ChatGPT to understand the meaning and context of the input and generate a coherent and appropriate response.

However, not all responses generated by ChatGPT are equally successful. In some cases, the model may generate responses that are irrelevant, offensive, or nonsensical. For example, if prompted with "What is the capital of France?" ChatGPT may respond with "My favorite fruit is apples." These types of responses can be frustrating for users and can undermine the credibility of the chatbot.

One challenge in understanding ChatGPT responses is that the model itself is seen as a black box – it can be difficult to interpret how it arrives at a particular response. However, there are some techniques that researchers use to gain insight into the workings of the model. One approach is to examine the attention weights produced by the model. Attention weights reflect the relative importance of different parts of the input in generating the output. By analyzing the attention weights, we can gain some insight into which parts of the input the model is focusing on and how it is processing the input. Another approach is to use adversarial testing to evaluate the model's response generation capabilities. Adversarial testing involves intentionally creating inputs that are difficult for the model to handle and examining the resulting outputs. For example, we may prompt the model with a statement that is semantically ambiguous or syntactically complex to see how it responds.

Despite best efforts, response coherence remains a challenge in generating high-quality responses. Because GPT-based models generate responses based on patterns and associations learned from a large corpus of text data, they may generate responses that are semantically or syntactically incoherent. For example, a GPT-based chatbot may generate a response that is completely unrelated to the question asked, or that uses incorrect grammar or sentence structure.

To evaluate the quality of chatbot responses, researchers have developed a number of metrics, including metrics that measure semantic similarity between the generated response and a reference response, as well as metrics that measure coherence and fluency. One commonly used metric for evaluating chatbot response quality is BLEU (Bilingual Evaluation Understudy), which measures the degree of overlap between the generated response and a set of reference responses.

To improve the coherence and fluency of chatbot responses, researchers have explored a range of techniques, including fine-tuning the pre-trained GPT model on specific datasets, incorporating external knowledge sources into the model, and using techniques like beam search and nucleus sampling to generate more diverse and coherent responses.

Beam search is a search algorithm that works by exploring multiple possible sequences of words in parallel. It starts by generating the most likely word at each step based on the probabilities of the next word given the previous words. It then keeps track of the most likely sequences and continues the process until the end of the sequence is reached. This allows the model to consider multiple possibilities for the next word, resulting in more coherent responses. Nucleus sampling, on the other hand, is a probabilistic technique that involves sampling from the top probability words. This probability is determined by a threshold parameter and is calculated based on the cumulative probability of the most likely words. The technique works by generating a probability distribution of the possible next words and then selecting a word from the set of words that make up the top probability mass. This allows the model to generate more diverse responses while still maintaining coherence. In essence, these techniques allow ChatGPT to consider multiple possible responses and choose the most coherent and diverse option, resulting in more natural and human-like conversations.

Another key challenge in generating high-quality chatbot responses is the issue of bias. Because GPT-based models are trained on large, diverse datasets of text data, they may inadvertently learn and reproduce biases present in the data. For example, a chatbot trained on a dataset that contains a disproportionate number of male-authored texts may be more likely to generate responses that reflect male perspectives and experiences.

To address these issues of bias, researchers have developed a number of techniques, such as counterfactual data augmentation, to mitigate the impact of bias in the training data. Counterfactual data augmentation is a technique used in machine learning to reduce the impact of bias in the training data. Essentially, it involves creating new, hypothetical data points that imagine what the world would look like if a particular bias did not exist. By adding these new data points to the training data, the model is encouraged to learn more diverse and fairer patterns, which can lead to more accurate and unbiased predictions.

To illustrate, imagine a machine learning model that is trained to determine whether a loan application should be approved or rejected. If the training data contains bias towards a certain group of people, such as women or minorities, the model may learn to discriminate against those groups in its predictions. Counterfactual data augmentation involves creating hypothetical data points that imagine what the world would look like if everyone had an equal chance of being approved for a loan, regardless of their gender, race, or other factors. By adding these hypothetical data points to the training data, the model is trained to make decisions that are more fair and unbiased.

Additionally, some researchers have explored the use of debiasing techniques, such as using generative adversarial networks (GANs) to generate synthetic training data that is more balanced and representative of diverse perspectives. The idea behind a GAN is to create a pair of artificial neural networks, one called the "generator" and the other called the "discriminator." The generator is trained to create new data that is similar to the real training data, while the discriminator is trained to tell the difference between the real data and the generated data. By having the generator and discriminator "compete" against each other, the generator gets better and better at creating synthetic data that is more and more similar to the real training data. This can help to create a more balanced and representative set of training data that includes diverse perspectives.

In conclusion, understanding and improving the quality of GPT-based chatbot responses is an important area of research that has the potential to transform the way we interact with machines. By addressing challenges related to response coherence and bias, and by exploring new approaches to evaluating and improving chatbot response quality, researchers are working to create more effective and engaging conversational agents that can better serve the needs of users in a wide range of domains.

# Chapter 5. Customizing ChatGPT

One of the most exciting features of ChatGPT is the ability to customize the model for specific use cases. This means that researchers and developers can fine-tune the model to improve its performance on a particular task or domain. In this chapter, we will explore the process of customizing ChatGPT and the various techniques that can be used to enhance its capabilities.

Before customizing a chatbot, it's important to determine the scope and purpose of the chatbot to ensure that it meets the specific needs of the user or organization. This involves understanding what tasks the chatbot will perform, who the intended users are, and what the desired outcome is. For example, if the chatbot is intended to provide customer support for a specific product, the scope might be limited to answering frequently asked questions and resolving common issues related to that product. In this case, the chatbot might be trained on a specific set of data related to that product, such as product manuals or customer support tickets.

On the other hand, if the chatbot is intended to be used in a medical setting, the scope might be broader and could include functions such as symptom checking, appointment scheduling, and prescription refills. In this case, the chatbot might need to be trained on a larger dataset of medical information and require more complex natural language processing capabilities.

Once the scope and purpose of the chatbot have been defined, the customization process can begin. This may involve selecting the appropriate platform, defining the chatbot's persona, and developing the conversation flow. It may also involve integrating the chatbot with other systems, such as customer relationship management software or payment systems.

Once you have determined the scope and purpose of your custom chatbot, the next step is to decide which aspects of ChatGPT you want to customize. Depending on your specific use case, you may want to simply fine-tune ChatGPT or develop an entirely new model.

## Fine-Tuning ChatGPT

Fine-tuning is the process of adapting a pre-trained model to a specific task or domain by updating its parameters on a smaller dataset. This is done by first initializing the model with the pre-trained weights and then training it on a task-specific dataset. The idea behind fine-tuning is that the pre-trained model has already learned a lot about the language and can be leveraged to solve related tasks.

The first step in fine-tuning ChatGPT is to select a task or domain that the model will be customized for. Fine-tuning involves taking the pre-trained model and training it further on a new dataset that is specific to the target domain or task. This allows the model to be adapted to the specific language patterns and vocabulary of the target domain, improving its performance for that particular task. This can range from simple tasks like text classification to more complex tasks like language translation. Once the task has been identified, a dataset must be prepared for the fine-tuning process. This dataset should be representative of the target domain or task and contain enough examples to enable the model to learn the patterns and characteristics of the data.

For example, imagine a healthcare chatbot that uses ChatGPT to interact with patients. The chatbot would need to be able to understand medical jargon and technical terms related to health, as well as the specific needs and concerns of patients. By fine-tuning ChatGPT on a dataset of medical conversations, the chatbot could be better equipped to understand and respond to patients' inquiries.

The next step is to load the pre-trained model and initialize it with the pre-trained weights. ChatGPT has been pre-trained on a large corpus of text data and can be fine-tuned on a variety of downstream tasks. The pre-trained model can be loaded using one of the popular deep learning frameworks like PyTorch or TensorFlow.

Once the pre-trained model has been loaded, the next step is to train it on the task-specific dataset. This is done by minimizing the loss function on the training set using gradient descent. The loss function is typically task-specific and can be chosen based on the nature of the task. For example, for a text classification task, the cross-entropy loss function can be used. What this means is that while a pre-trained model can recognize patterns and relationships between the data, to use it for a specific task, like identifying if an email is spam or not, the model needs to be trained on a smaller set of data that is specific to that task.

To do this, the model is "fine-tuned" by adjusting its internal parameters through a process called "gradient descent," which means minimizing a "loss function" that measures how well the model is doing on the task-specific dataset. The loss function is chosen based on the nature of the task, and it calculates how far the model's predictions are from the actual labels of the data.

For example, if the task is to classify text as positive or negative sentiment, the loss function used could be the "cross-entropy" loss function. This function measures the difference between the predicted probability of each class and the true label, and tries to minimize this difference by updating the parameters of the model until it can accurately predict whether a given text has a positive or negative sentiment.

During the fine-tuning process, the hyperparameters of the model can also be tuned. These include the learning rate, batch size, and number of training epochs. Tuning these hyperparameters can significantly impact the performance of the model on the task-specific dataset. The learning rate determines how quickly the model adapts to the task-specific dataset, while the batch size controls how many data samples are used in each iteration of the training process. The number of training epochs determines how many times the model is trained on the entire dataset.

Choosing appropriate values for these hyperparameters is important as it can impact the training time, model accuracy, and the ability to generalize to new data. For example, a small learning rate may result in the model being under-trained, while a large learning rate may cause the model to overfit the training data. Similarly, a large batch size can lead to a faster training process but may cause the model to generalize poorly to new data. Finding the right combination of hyperparameters is often an iterative process that requires testing different values and evaluating their impact on the model's performance.

Another popular approach to fine-tuning ChatGPT is to use transfer learning. Transfer learning is a technique that involves taking a pre-trained model and adapting it to a new task. The idea behind transfer learning is that the pre-trained model has already learned useful representations of language, which can be adapted to the new task. There are several ways to use transfer learning to fine-tune ChatGPT. One approach is to take the pre-trained model and add a new output layer that is specific to your task. This new output layer can then be trained on your domain-specific dataset. Another approach is to freeze certain layers of the pre-trained model and only train the new layers that are specific to your task. This can help to preserve the useful representations learned by the pre-trained model.

Another way to customize ChatGPT is to modify the architecture of the model. This can be done by adding or removing layers, changing the activation functions, or adjusting the size of the layers. Modifying the architecture can be a more advanced technique, as it requires a deeper understanding of the inner workings of the model. However, it can also lead to significant improvements in the model's performance.

In addition to fine-tuning and modifying the architecture, there are several other techniques for customizing ChatGPT. One such technique is to use data augmentation. Data augmentation involves generating new data by applying transformations to your existing dataset. For example, you can rotate or crop images, or add noise to audio recordings. By generating new data, you can increase the diversity of your dataset and improve the model's ability to generalize to new examples.

Another technique for customizing ChatGPT is to use ensembling. Ensembling involves combining the predictions of multiple models to produce a final prediction. This can help to improve the robustness and accuracy of the model, especially when dealing with noisy or uncertain data.

You may also find that you have a need to re-configure the input/output mechanisms. This can involve modifying the user interface, implementing additional input sources (such as audio or video), or customizing the response generation process to suit your specific use case. For example, you may want to modify the response generation process to prioritize certain topics or to incorporate specific branding or marketing messages.

In some cases, modifying the existing model does not provide the specific outputs you are looking for, and instead, you need to look at training a specific model for your specific needs.

## Training a new model

Another approach to customizing ChatGPT is to train a new model from scratch using a custom dataset. This approach is more complex and time-consuming than fine-tuning, but it allows for greater control over the model architecture and training process. Training a new model involves selecting an appropriate architecture and hyperparameters, preparing a dataset, and training the model using backpropagation. To do this, the first step is to decide what kind of pattern recognition "architecture" the model should have. This could be, for example, a neural network, which is a type of mathematical model inspired by the way neurons in the brain work. Next, the "hyperparameters" of the model need to be selected, which are the same settings discussed earlier. These settings control how the model learns from the data, such as how fast it should adjust its parameters or how many "layers" it should have. Once the architecture and hyperparameters have been selected, a dataset needs to be prepared. This means collecting or creating a set of data that is large enough for the model to learn from. The data is usually split into two parts: a training set and a test set. The training set is used to teach the model, while the test set is used to evaluate how well it has learned. Finally, the model is trained using a process called "backpropagation," which involves repeatedly exposing the model to the training data, calculating the errors it makes, and adjusting its parameters to reduce those errors. The goal is to train the model until it can accurately recognize patterns in new data that it hasn't seen before.

One use case for training a new model might be creating a chatbot for a specific company or product. By training a new model on customer support conversations related to that product, the chatbot could be better equipped to answer questions and resolve issues specific to that product. Another use case might be creating a chatbot for a specific language or dialect that is not well-represented in the pre-trained models.

However, training a new model from scratch requires a significant amount of data, computing power, and expertise. It also runs the risk of overfitting the model to the training data, resulting in poor generalization to new data. This means the model becomes too good at recognizing patterns in the specific data it was trained on, but it may not perform well on new data it hasn't seen before. For example, if a model is trained to recognize dogs in pictures but has only seen pictures of a specific breed, it may not recognize dogs of other breeds.

## Challenges and considerations

Customizing ChatGPT can be a powerful tool for improving the performance of chatbots and other NLP applications, but it also presents some challenges and considerations. One of the main challenges is finding a suitable dataset for fine-tuning or training a new model. The dataset must be representative of the target domain or task, and it must be large and diverse enough to train a high-quality model. For instance, if you want to train a model to recognize faces, you need a dataset of many different faces from different races, ages, genders, and lighting conditions.

In addition to being representative, the dataset must also be large enough to ensure that the model has seen enough examples to generalize well. The size of the dataset required depends on the complexity of the problem and the size of the model. For instance, if you want to train a model to detect fraud in financial transactions, you may need a dataset containing millions of examples of both fraudulent and legitimate transactions. The dataset must also be labeled correctly so that the model can learn from it. For example, in the case of fraud detection, each transaction in the dataset would be labeled as either fraudulent or legitimate. It's also important to ensure that the dataset is balanced, meaning it contains roughly equal numbers of examples for each class. For example, if you want to train a model to recognize cats and dogs, the dataset should have roughly the same number of cat images and dog images. If the dataset is unbalanced, the model may be biased towards the class with more examples.

Another challenge is avoiding bias and fairness issues in the customized model. For example, if a chatbot is trained on a dataset that only includes conversations from a certain demographic group, the chatbot may be less effective or even discriminatory towards other groups. It is important to ensure that the dataset is diverse and representative of the target audience.

Privacy is also a consideration when customizing ChatGPT, as training data may contain sensitive or personally identifiable information. It is important to take appropriate measures to protect the privacy and security of the training data, such as using data encryption or de-identification techniques.

## Conclusion

Once you have determined which aspects of ChatGPT to customize, the next step is to actually implement the modifications. Depending on the complexity of the changes, this may involve modifying the source code of the language model, developing new input/output modules, or integrating third-party tools or APIs. It is important to thoroughly test the modified system to ensure that it performs as intended and does not introduce any unintended errors or vulnerabilities.

One key benefit of customizing ChatGPT is that it allows organizations to create chatbots that are tailored to their specific needs and requirements. This can result in more efficient and effective communication with customers, clients, or other stakeholders. Custom chatbots can also help organizations to differentiate themselves from competitors and to reinforce their brand messaging and values.

However, it is important to keep in mind that customizing ChatGPT can be a complex and resource-intensive process. Depending on the scope of the modifications, it may require significant expertise in natural language processing, machine learning, and software engineering. Organizations considering custom chatbots should carefully weigh the potential benefits against the costs and risks associated with developing and maintaining a custom solution.

Overall, customizing ChatGPT offers organizations a powerful tool for creating chatbots that are tailored to their specific needs and requirements. By carefully selecting training data, modifying the language model architecture, and configuring the input/output mechanisms, organizations can create chatbots that are more effective, efficient, and tailored to their specific use case. While customizing ChatGPT can be a complex and resource-intensive process, it offers significant potential benefits in terms of improved communication, differentiation, and branding.

# Part III: Advanced Topics

## Chapter 6. NLP and Deep Learning Basics

To start, it is important to understand the basics of Natural Language Processing (NLP) and Deep Learning. NLP is a branch of artificial intelligence that deals with the interaction between computers and humans in natural language, whereas deep learning is a subset of machine learning that involves neural networks with multiple layers. Deep learning has been a key driving force in recent advancements in NLP. Let's take a closer look at each.

Natural Language Processing (NLP) is a field of computer science that focuses on the interactions between humans and computers using natural language. In NLP, the main goal is to teach computers to understand, interpret and generate human language. NLP models are trained using large amounts of text data and rely on a variety of techniques to extract meaning from natural language. These techniques include part-of-speech tagging, named entity recognition, sentiment analysis, machine translation, and question answering, among others. The ultimate goal is to create models that can understand and respond to natural language in a way that is similar to human conversation.

One of the key challenges in NLP is dealing with the inherent ambiguity and complexity of natural language. For example, many words can have multiple meanings depending on the context, and sentences can have multiple valid interpretations. NLP techniques use a variety of methods to disambiguate and interpret natural language, including statistical methods, machine learning algorithms, and rule-based systems.

1. Statistical Methods: These methods involve analyzing large volumes of text data and using statistical models to identify patterns and relationships. For example, one statistical method is to use frequency analysis to identify the most common words or phrases in a text.

2. Machine Learning Algorithms: These methods involve training a machine learning model on a large dataset of text to enable it to recognize patterns and relationships in natural language. For example, a machine learning algorithm can be trained to identify the sentiment of a text as positive, negative, or neutral.

3. Rule-based Systems: These methods involve using a set of predefined rules to analyze and process natural language. These rules can be based on linguistic or semantic rules, such as the rules that govern English grammar. For example, a rule-based system can be used to identify named entities in a text, such as people, places, and organizations.

Overall, NLP techniques use a combination of these methods to analyze and interpret natural language, enabling machines to perform tasks such as text classification, sentiment analysis, and language translation.

Deep learning, on the other hand, is a machine learning technique that involves the use of artificial neural networks with multiple layers. These networks are capable of learning complex representations of data by processing it through layers of interconnected nodes. The layers closest to the input data are responsible for capturing basic features, while deeper layers are responsible for more abstract and complex representations. Essentially, deep learning models complex relationships in data.

Deep learning has proven to be particularly effective in NLP tasks such as language modeling, machine translation, sentiment analysis, and speech recognition. Deep learning models are typically trained on large datasets using a technique called backpropagation, which involves iteratively adjusting the model's weights based on the errors it makes on the training data.

One of the key benefits of deep learning is its ability to automatically learn useful features from raw data, without the need for manual feature engineering. This makes deep learning particularly well-suited for NLP, where traditional feature engineering approaches can be difficult and time-consuming.

There are several types of neural networks commonly used in NLP, including feedforward neural networks, recurrent neural networks (RNNs), and convolutional neural networks (CNNs).

1.  Feedforward Neural Networks: These are the simplest type of neural network, where

information flows in only one direction - from the input layer, through one or more hidden layers, and to the output layer. Feedforward neural networks are often used for simple NLP tasks, such as text classification.

2. Recurrent Neural Networks (RNNs): These neural networks are designed to process sequential data, such as text. RNNs have a "memory" component that allows them to remember information from previous time steps, which is useful for tasks such as language modeling, machine translation, and speech recognition.

3. Convolutional Neural Networks (CNNs): These neural networks are commonly used for image recognition, but they can also be applied to NLP tasks such as text classification. CNNs use filters that slide over the input data, capturing features at different levels of abstraction. They are particularly useful for tasks that require analyzing local features within a sequence, such as part-of-speech tagging.

Overall, the choice of neural network architecture depends on the specific NLP task at hand, as well as the size and complexity of the dataset. Researchers and practitioners often experiment with different neural network architectures to find the most effective approach for their particular task.

In recent years, several deep learning architectures have been developed specifically for NLP tasks. One of the most popular is the transformer architecture, which was first introduced in the paper "Attention is All You Need" by Vaswani et al. (2017). The transformer architecture uses a self-attention mechanism to allow each position in the input sequence to attend to all other positions, enabling the model to learn global relationships between the input tokens.

This transformer architecture has been widely used in many state-of-the-art NLP models, including BERT (Bidirectional Encoder Representations from Transformers), GPT (Generative Pretrained Transformer), and T5 (Text-to-Text Transfer Transformer). These models have achieved impressive results on a variety of NLP benchmarks, including machine translation, question answering, and language modeling.

To understand how NLP and deep learning can be used together, consider the example of language translation. The traditional approach to language translation involves using rule-based systems that rely on pre-defined grammatical rules to translate text from one language to another. However, these systems often struggle with the nuances of language and fail to capture the context of the text being translated.

In contrast, deep learning models can learn to translate between languages by processing large amounts of text data and learning to identify patterns and relationships between words and phrases in different languages. The Transformer model, in particular, has been shown to be effective for language translation, as it can process entire sequences of input text at once and capture the context of the text being translated.

In addition to language translation, deep learning models have also been used for a variety of other NLP tasks, including sentiment analysis, named entity recognition, and text classification. These models have achieved state-of-the-art performance on many benchmarks and have demonstrated the potential for significant advancements in the field of NLP.

However, it is important to note that deep learning models also have their limitations. They require large amounts of high-quality training data to achieve good performance, and they can be computationally expensive to train and run. Additionally, these models can sometimes be difficult to interpret, which can make it challenging to understand why a particular decision was made.

In all, NLP and deep learning are two powerful technologies that are transforming the field of artificial intelligence. They offer a wide range of applications for improving communication between humans and computers, and they have the potential to revolutionize the way we interact with machines. While there are still challenges to be addressed, such as the need for more robust data and interpretability of models, the future of NLP and deep learning is bright, and we can expect to see many exciting developments in this field in the years to come.

# Chapter 7. Training Your Own ChatGPT Model

To train a ChatGPT model, you will need to follow a number of steps, including selecting and preparing a dataset, setting up a training environment, and fine-tuning the model. Let's take a closer look at each of these steps.

## Selecting and preparing a dataset

The first step in training your own ChatGPT model is to select a suitable dataset. The quality and size of your dataset will have a significant impact on the performance of your model, so it is important to choose carefully. This dataset can be obtained from a variety of sources, such as web pages, books, or other online resources. Your dataset should be representative of the kind of text that your ChatGPT model will be expected to generate. For example, if you are building a chatbot for customer service, you may want to use a dataset of customer inquiries and responses. If you are building a model for generating creative writing, you may want to use a dataset of novels or short stories.

One important consideration when training your own ChatGPT model is the ethical and social implications of the technology. As with any AI technology, there is a risk of bias or other ethical issues, which can be exacerbated when training a model on a dataset that may contain biased or problematic content. To mitigate these risks, it is important to carefully consider the dataset used to train the model, and to take steps to ensure that the model is as unbiased and fair as possible. This may involve carefully selecting the sources of data used to train the model, or applying techniques such as adversarial training to expose and eliminate bias in the model.

Once the dataset has been obtained, the next step is to preprocess the data to prepare it for training. This involves several steps, such as cleaning the data by removing irrelevant or unwanted text, tokenizing the data by breaking it into individual words or subwords, and encoding the data in a way that can be used by the model.

## Setting up a training environment

The next step is to set up a training environment for your ChatGPT model. This will typically involve using a deep learning framework, such as PyTorch or TensorFlow, and setting up a computing environment that can handle the large amounts of data and computation required for training.

In order to create and train your own ChatGPT model, you will need to make sure your computer has the right tools and software. This includes choosing the right type of hardware, like a powerful graphics card called a GPU or a specialized chip called a TPU. You will also need to install specific software, including a type of computer program called a deep learning framework and other related libraries, to make sure everything runs smoothly. This can involve some technical setup, but there are many resources available to help guide you through the process.

The next step is to actually train the model. This involves using the preprocessed data to train the model using an algorithm such as the transformer model. This can be a computationally intensive process, requiring significant processing power and time, depending on the size of the dataset and complexity of the model. There are several tools and platforms available for training your own ChatGPT model. Some popular options include the Hugging Face Transformers library, which provides a variety of pre-trained models and tools for training new models, and Google Cloud's AI Platform, which provides a range of machine learning tools and services, including support for training ChatGPT models.

**Fine-tuning the model**

Once you have prepared your dataset and set up your training environment, the next step is to fine-tune your ChatGPT model. Fine-tuning involves taking a pre-trained model and adapting it to your specific dataset and task. There are several techniques for fine-tuning a ChatGPT model, including transfer learning, where the model is trained on a similar but different dataset before being fine-tuned on the target dataset, and gradual unfreezing, where the model is unfrozen layer by layer to allow for more targeted fine-tuning. During the fine-tuning process, you will need to experiment with different hyperparameters, such as the learning rate, batch size, and number of training epochs, to achieve the best performance.

Think of hyperparameters as the settings you can change to make sure the model is learning in the best possible way. For example, the learning rate refers to how quickly the model should adjust its predictions based on new information. The batch size refers to how many examples the model should process at once before updating its parameters, which can affect how accurately it learns. The number of training epochs refers to how many times the model should go through the training data. By experimenting with these settings, you can find the best combination to make the model perform as well as possible.

**Validation and testing**

Once you have fine-tuned your ChatGPT model, the next step is to validate and test it. Validation involves checking the performance of the model on a validation set, which is a subset of the data that was not used during training. Testing involves evaluating the performance of the model on a separate test set, which is a subset of the data that was not used during training or validation. This helps to ensure that the model is not overfitting to the training data, and that it is able to generalize to new data.

**Conclusion**

Training your own ChatGPT model can be a challenging but rewarding process. By selecting a suitable dataset, setting up a training environment, fine-tuning the model, and validating and testing its performance, you can create a customized ChatGPT model that is tailored to your specific needs and applications. It is important to keep in mind that training a ChatGPT model requires a significant amount of computational resources and expertise in deep learning. However, with the right tools and knowledge, anyone can train their own ChatGPT model and take advantage of the power of natural language processing for a wide range of applications. It is also important to consider the ethical implications of training and deploying a ChatGPT model, such as the potential for bias and the impact on privacy and security. It is essential to follow best practices in data collection and cleaning, as well as to implement debiasing techniques and other measures to ensure that the model is fair and representative. Additionally, it is crucial to adhere to ethical guidelines and regulations, such as obtaining informed consent and protecting sensitive information. By taking a responsible and informed approach to training and using ChatGPT models, we can unlock their full potential while minimizing the risks and challenges they may pose.

# Chapter 8. Scaling ChatGPT for Enterprise

In this chapter, we will discuss how to scale ChatGPT for enterprise-level applications. As with any AI application, the performance of ChatGPT can vary greatly depending on the size of the data it has access to, the amount of computing power available, and the quality of the training data. Scaling ChatGPT for enterprise requires a thoughtful approach to data management, infrastructure, and deployment.

**Data Management**

One of the key challenges in scaling ChatGPT for enterprise is managing the large volumes of data required for training and inference. The quality of the data used to train the model is critical to its performance. The data must be diverse and representative of the domain in which the chatbot will operate. In addition, the data must be labeled and annotated in a way that allows the model to understand the nuances of human language.

When training a machine learning model like ChatGPT, it's important to have a lot of data to feed into the model so it can learn from it. However, managing such a large amount of data can be a challenge, which is why there are some strategies that can be used to simplify the process. One strategy is to use a distributed file system, such as Hadoop, which is a type of file system that can distribute data across multiple machines. This can make the processing of data much faster and more efficient. Another strategy is to pre-process the data before feeding it into the model. This can involve removing any noise or irrelevant information that may interfere with the model's ability to learn from the data. By pre-processing the data, the model can focus on the most important information and produce better results. Lastly, data augmentation can be used to increase the diversity of the training set. This can involve adding synonyms or similar phrases to the training set, which can help the model understand different ways in which a particular concept can be expressed. By increasing the variety of data that the model is exposed to, it can become more robust and effective in generating responses.

## Infrastructure

Scaling ChatGPT requires significant computing resources. This can be a challenge for enterprises that do not have the necessary infrastructure in place. Fortunately, cloud-based infrastructure services, such as Amazon Web Services (AWS) and Google Cloud Platform (GCP), make it easy to scale compute resources up and down as needed. To get started, the first step is to choose a cloud provider that meets the needs of the organization, which involves several considerations, such as the cost, security, availability, and scalability of the provider. Organizations should assess their budget and determine the cost of using a cloud provider, including any potential hidden costs such as network egress fees or data transfer costs. Security is another important consideration, and organizations should ensure that the cloud provider has appropriate security measures in place, such as encryption, access control, and data protection policies. The availability of the cloud provider is also important, and organizations should choose a provider with a high uptime percentage to minimize downtime and disruption to services. Finally, scalability is a key consideration, and organizations should choose a provider that can scale up or down to meet changing demand for computational resources.

Once an organization has selected a cloud provider, the next step is to choose an instance type that can meet the requirements of the ChatGPT workload. The cloud provider typically offers a range of instance types, which can vary in terms of compute capacity, memory, storage, and network bandwidth. In the case of ChatGPT, a GPU-based instance is recommended due to the significant compute requirements of the model. GPUs are particularly well-suited for deep learning workloads because they can perform large-scale parallel computations, which are necessary for training neural networks quickly and efficiently.

When we want to use a cloud provider to train a ChatGPT model, we have to select a type of computer that can handle the amount of computing power we need to train the model. Amazon Web Services (AWS) is one cloud provider that offers different types of these computers, which they call "instances". These instances have different types of computer processors that can handle different amounts of work. For training ChatGPT, we recommend using an instance that has a special type of processor called an NVIDIA GPU, because these are best suited for the type of math that is required to train the model. The P3, P3dn, and G4 instance families are all examples of instances that have NVIDIA GPUs, but they each have different amounts of memory and different types of processors, so we need to choose the one that best fits our needs. The P3dn instance type is especially useful for large-scale training and data transfers because it has very fast network connections.

When selecting an instance type, it is important to consider the specific requirements of the ChatGPT workload. For example, larger models or datasets may require more memory or storage capacity, and may benefit from higher network bandwidth. It is also important to consider the cost implications of each instance type, as more powerful instances can be significantly more expensive than smaller ones.

In addition to selecting the right instance type, it is also important to configure the instance properly to ensure that it can effectively run the ChatGPT workload. This may involve installing and configuring the necessary deep learning frameworks, such as TensorFlow or PyTorch, as well as any other libraries or dependencies that are required for the particular use case. It is also important to ensure that the instance has sufficient storage and is properly networked to the rest of the infrastructure.

## Deployment

Once the infrastructure is in place and the data has been collected and pre-processed, the next step is to deploy the ChatGPT model. This can be done using a variety of deployment strategies, depending on the needs of the organization.

One common approach is to make it available as a RESTful API, which stands for Representational State Transfer Application Programming Interface. A RESTful API is a web-based interface that allows other applications to access the model's predictions by sending requests to the API and receiving the responses. Deploying a model as a RESTful API can provide a lot of flexibility and ease of use. Because the model is deployed as a web service, it can be accessed by a wide range of other applications that are designed to work with RESTful APIs. These might include web applications, mobile apps, or even other machine learning models that need to make use of ChatGPT's output. To use a ChatGPT model deployed as a RESTful API, an application would typically send a request to the API that includes the input text that needs to be processed. The API would then use the deployed model to generate a response, and send it back to the requesting application. The requesting application can then use the response as needed. The use of a RESTful API to deploy a machine learning model like ChatGPT can provide many benefits, including ease of use, flexibility, and scalability. By making the model available as a web service, it becomes much easier for other applications to make use of its capabilities. Additionally, because the API can be scaled up or down as needed, it can be a good option for handling large volumes of requests from multiple applications.

Another approach is to deploy the model using containerization technologies, such as Docker. Containerization technologies provide a way to package software into a container that includes all the necessary dependencies and configuration, allowing it to be easily deployed on different systems. In the case of deploying a ChatGPT model, Docker can be used to package the model and its associated software, such as the deep learning framework and dependencies, into a single container. This container can then be run on any system that supports Docker, such as a local machine, a cloud instance, or a Kubernetes cluster.[1] To deploy a ChatGPT model using Docker, the first step is to create a Docker image that includes the necessary software and dependencies. This image can be built using a Dockerfile, which specifies the steps required to build the image. Once the image is built, it can be run as a container using the Docker run command, which starts a new container instance from the image. The container can be configured to expose

1. Kubernetes is an open-source container orchestration platform used to manage and deploy containerized applications. A Kubernetes cluster is a group of nodes, or servers, that run containerized applications and are managed by the Kubernetes master. The Kubernetes master acts as the control plane for the cluster, managing and coordinating the deployment and scaling of containerized applications across the nodes. Each node in the cluster runs the Kubernetes agent, which communicates with the master to receive instructions on how to manage the containers running on that node. Using a Kubernetes cluster provides several benefits, such as high availability, scalability, and automated management of containerized applications. It also allows for easy deployment and management of applications across multiple environments, such as on-premises data centers, public cloud providers, and hybrid environments.

the model as a RESTful API or to serve the model using other deployment strategies. Overall, using Docker to deploy ChatGPT models can simplify the deployment process and make it easy to move the model between different environments.

Containerization provides several benefits for deploying ChatGPT models. First, it simplifies the deployment process by ensuring that all the necessary software and dependencies are included in the container, eliminating the need to manually install and configure them on the target system. Second, containers provide a consistent runtime environment, ensuring that the model will behave the same way regardless of the system on which it is deployed. Third, containers are lightweight and can be easily moved between different environments, making it easy to deploy the model on different systems as needed.

## Monitoring and Maintenance

Once the ChatGPT model has been deployed, it is important to monitor its performance and maintain its accuracy over time. This can be done using a variety of monitoring and maintenance strategies.

When deploying a machine learning model, it's important to have a system in place to monitor its performance over time. One way to do this is by using metrics to track the model's accuracy and other performance indicators. Accuracy refers to the proportion of predictions that the model got right compared to the actual outcomes. Precision, on the other hand, measures the proportion of true positive predictions among all positive predictions, while recall measures the proportion of true positive predictions among all actual positive outcomes. Other metrics that can be used include F1 score, which is the harmonic mean of precision and recall, and area under the curve (AUC), which measures the model's ability to distinguish between positive and negative outcomes.

By monitoring these metrics over time, it's possible to identify issues with the model's performance and make adjustments to improve its accuracy and other performance indicators. For example, if the accuracy or precision of the model starts to decline, it may be an indication that the model is overfitting to the training data and may need to be retrained with additional data. Alternatively, if the recall is low, it may indicate that the model is missing important patterns in the data, and additional features or more complex algorithms may be needed to improve its performance.

It's also important to consider the tradeoff between different metrics. For example, increasing the accuracy of the model may come at the cost of reducing its precision, and vice versa. Balancing different performance metrics can be a complex task that requires careful consideration of the specific use case and requirements.

Another approach is to use continuous integration and continuous deployment (CI/CD) pipelines to automate the deployment and maintenance of the model. Continuous integration and continuous deployment (CI/CD) are software development practices that aim to streamline the software development and deployment process. The goal is to automate the process of building, testing, and deploying software changes, including machine learning models, so that it is faster and more reliable. In the context of deploying ChatGPT models, a CI/CD pipeline can be used to automate the deployment and maintenance of the model. This involves setting up a pipeline that includes various stages, such as building the model, testing it, and deploying it to a production environment. The pipeline can be triggered automatically whenever changes are made to the model or its dependencies, such as the training data or hyperparameters. When a change is detected, the pipeline will automatically build and test the model, and if everything passes, it will deploy the new version of the model to the production environment. By using a CI/CD pipeline, the deployment process can be streamlined, and the model can be updated quickly and reliably. This approach is popular because it reduces the risk of errors and ensures that the model is always up-to-date and performing at its best.

## Conclusion

Scaling ChatGPT for enterprise requires a thoughtful approach to data management, infrastructure, and deployment. By following best practices for data management, infrastructure, deployment, and monitoring and maintenance, it is possible to create a powerful and accurate chatbot that can meet the needs of any organization. With the increasing demand for conversational AI in the enterprise, ChatGPT is a powerful tool that can help organizations enhance their customer service, improve their operational efficiency, and gain valuable insights into their customers' needs and preferences. However, scaling ChatGPT for enterprise requires careful planning and execution. This includes selecting the right dataset, choosing a suitable hardware configuration, and deploying the model in a way that is flexible, scalable, and easy to maintain. It is also important to monitor the performance of the model over time and make adjustments as necessary to ensure that it continues to meet the organization's needs. With the right tools and expertise, any organization can leverage the power of ChatGPT to create a chatbot that delivers exceptional customer experiences and drives business success.

In the chapters that follow, we will take a closer look at three common uses for ChatGPT in an enterprise setting: customer service, education, and creative writing.

# Part IV: Applications

## Chapter 9. ChatGPT for Customer Service

Customer service is one of the most critical areas where companies interact with their customers. Traditionally, customer service has relied on human agents to handle customer queries and resolve issues. However, with the rise of NLP technologies, chatbots and virtual assistants have become popular tools for customer service. ChatGPT is one such technology that can be used to develop highly efficient and effective chatbots for customer service.

One of the significant advantages of using ChatGPT for customer service is the ability to handle a large volume of customer queries simultaneously. ChatGPT can analyze and process customer queries quickly and accurately, without any delay in response time. This is a significant advantage over traditional customer service, where human agents may have to put customers on hold or transfer them to another agent to resolve their issues.

To use ChatGPT for customer service, the first step is to create a dataset of customer queries and corresponding responses. This dataset should be carefully curated to ensure that it covers all the possible customer queries and responses that may arise during a customer service interaction. The dataset should also be diverse enough to cover different types of customers and their preferences.

Once the dataset is created, the next step is to fine-tune the pre-trained ChatGPT model to learn from the dataset. Fine-tuning the model involves training it on the dataset of customer queries and responses, adjusting the model's parameters to optimize its performance on this particular task. This process can take some time, but the resulting model will be highly customized for customer service interactions.

In addition to these technical considerations, there are also important ethical and social implications to consider when using ChatGPT for customer service. One of the critical considerations in using ChatGPT for customer service is the need for ethical and responsible AI. Customer service interactions can be sensitive and may involve private or personal information. Therefore, it is essential to ensure that the chatbot is programmed to respect customer privacy and protect their data. Companies must also ensure that the chatbot is not used for malicious purposes or to manipulate customer behavior.

There are also concerns about the potential for bias and discrimination, especially in cases where the training data reflects pre-existing social and cultural biases. Additionally, there is a risk that ChatGPT may not fully understand or be able to respond appropriately to the emotional or social nuances of customer interactions, which can result in negative experiences for customers.

To address these concerns, it is important to engage in ongoing monitoring and evaluation of ChatGPT's performance, both in terms of technical accuracy and ethical considerations. This can include regular auditing of the training data and models to identify and address any biases or inaccuracies, as well as ongoing training and support for customer service representatives who may be working with ChatGPT to ensure that they are equipped with the knowledge and skills necessary to provide high-quality, ethical customer service.

Another consideration is the need to design the chatbot's user interface and user experience carefully. The chatbot should be easy to use and navigate, with a clear and concise interface. It should also be designed to handle customer queries quickly and accurately, without any confusion or delays in response time. The chatbot should be able to anticipate customer needs and provide relevant and personalized recommendations. While ChatGPT can be an effective tool for automating routine or simple interactions, there may be cases where customers prefer or require a more personalized or human touch. In these cases, it may be necessary to integrate ChatGPT with other tools or technologies, such as live chat tools or customer relationship management (CRM) systems, to provide a more holistic and personalized customer service experience. This integration allows the chatbot to access customer information and history to provide more personalized recommendations and resolutions to their queries.

One of the significant advantages of using ChatGPT for customer service is the ability to learn from customer interactions and feedback. Chatbots can be programmed to collect and analyze customer feedback to improve their performance continually. This feedback can be used to optimize the chatbot's responses, customize its recommendations, and improve its overall performance.

Finally, it is important to consider the potential impact of ChatGPT on the broader customer service industry. As more companies adopt chatbots and other AI-powered tools, there is a risk that the quality of customer service may suffer if these tools are not properly designed and implemented. To ensure that the use of ChatGPT and other AI-powered tools leads to better customer experiences, it is important to engage in ongoing research and development, and to work closely with stakeholders and end-users to identify and address any challenges or concerns that may arise.

One example of using ChatGPT for customer service is in the financial industry. Banks and other financial institutions can use ChatGPT-powered chatbots to handle customer queries related to account balances, transactions, loans, and other financial products. The chatbot can provide personalized recommendations and help customers navigate through complex financial jargon.

Another example is in the e-commerce industry. Online retailers can use ChatGPT-powered chatbots to help customers with their orders, returns, and refunds. The chatbot can provide customers with personalized recommendations based on their purchase history and browsing behavior.

In conclusion, ChatGPT has the potential to revolutionize the field of customer service by enabling companies to automate routine or simple interactions, while also providing a more personalized and efficient customer experience. However, to fully realize these benefits, it is important to consider the technical, ethical, and social implications of using ChatGPT for customer service, and to engage in ongoing monitoring, evaluation, and improvement to ensure that ChatGPT is deployed in a way that is both effective and ethical. With the right approach and the right tools, ChatGPT can be a powerful tool for driving innovation, improving customer experiences, and delivering better business outcomes.

# Chapter 10. ChatGPT for Education

In recent years, natural language processing (NLP) technologies have found increasing use in the education sector, where they are being applied in a range of areas, from language learning to student support and counseling. ChatGPT is one such NLP technology that has the potential to transform the way education is delivered, enabling personalized learning experiences, enhancing communication between students and educators, and improving the efficiency of administrative tasks. In this section, we will explore the different ways in which ChatGPT can be used in education and the benefits it can bring to the sector.

## Language Learning

One of the most promising applications of ChatGPT in education is language learning. For example, ChatGPT can be used to create conversational agents that simulate real-life conversations in the target language, allowing students to practice their conversational skills. These agents can be designed to converse on a range of topics, from everyday topics like food and weather to more specialized topics like business or travel. ChatGPT can also be used to create language learning games that use natural language processing to provide feedback and corrections to students as they play.

Furthermore, ChatGPT can help educators tailor language learning experiences to individual student needs. With its ability to adapt to user inputs and generate customized responses, ChatGPT can be used to create personalized language learning experiences that are tailored to each student's unique strengths and weaknesses. Additionally, by tracking student progress over time and analyzing their performance data, ChatGPT can be used to provide insights into areas where students may need additional support or practice. Overall, ChatGPT has the potential to revolutionize the way language learning is approached and can help students achieve higher levels of proficiency in a more engaging and interactive manner.

## Personalized Learning

Another area where ChatGPT can have a significant impact is in personalized learning. Personalized learning is an approach to education that tailors instruction and learning experiences to the individual needs and preferences of each student. The goal is to create a more effective and engaging learning experience by providing students with materials that are tailored to their unique learning style, interests, and pace. ChatGPT's ability to analyze large amounts of data and generate responses based on that data makes it well-suited for creating personalized learning experiences. By analyzing data on each student's performance, preferences, and behavior, ChatGPT can identify areas where they need more help and create learning materials that are designed to address those areas. This approach can help to keep students engaged and motivated, as they are more likely to be interested in and challenged by materials that are relevant to their personal interests and goals. In addition, personalized learning has been shown to improve learning outcomes and student achievement.

## Student Support and Counseling

ChatGPT can also be used to provide support and counseling to students, particularly in situations where human counselors are not available or accessible. The use of ChatGPT in providing support and counseling to students has the potential to greatly improve access to mental health services, especially for those who may feel stigmatized or uncomfortable seeking help from a human counselor. Chatbots can create a safe and anonymous space for students to discuss their concerns and receive advice and guidance without fear of judgement. In addition, ChatGPT can help address the issue of counselor shortage in schools and universities, where demand for mental health services often exceeds the capacity of available resources. By providing an additional resource for students to access support, ChatGPT-powered chatbots can help fill this gap and ensure that students receive the assistance they need in a timely manner. However, it is important to note that while chatbots can provide valuable support, they are not a substitute for human counselors or mental health professionals, and should be used as a complementary resource.

## Administrative Tasks

In addition to the examples mentioned earlier, ChatGPT can also be used to streamline other administrative tasks in the education sector. For instance, chatbots can be used to automate the process of scheduling and rescheduling classes and exams. This can save educators and administrative staff time and effort, and ensure that students receive timely updates and notifications. Another example is using ChatGPT to automate the process of creating and distributing educational materials. For example, chatbots can be used to generate quiz questions, practice exercises, and other learning materials based on the student's progress and performance. This can help ensure that students are provided with appropriate learning materials that are tailored to their individual needs and abilities.

Chatbots can also be used to provide feedback and support to students outside of traditional classroom settings. For instance, chatbots can be used to provide support to students studying for standardized tests such as the SAT or GRE, providing them with personalized advice and guidance on how to improve their scores. Additionally, chatbots can be used to assist students with college applications and admissions, providing them with information and resources on how to prepare for the application process, and guiding them through the various steps involved.

ChatGPT has also been used by educators to develop fun, in-class activities, simulations, and exercises based on provided topics or learning objectives. ChatGPT has been used to role-play one side of a debate, and provide feedback and facilitate discussion within the classroom based on student inputs.

Overall, the use of ChatGPT in the education sector has the potential to revolutionize the way that students learn and interact with educational institutions. By automating administrative tasks, providing personalized learning experiences, and offering support to students in new and innovative ways, ChatGPT-powered chatbots can help students reach their full potential and succeed in their academic pursuits.

## Challenges and Limitations

While ChatGPT has the potential to bring significant benefits to the education sector, there are also several challenges and limitations that need to be addressed. One of the main challenges is ensuring that the chatbots are able to provide accurate and appropriate responses to students. This requires training the chatbots on a large dataset of relevant material and constantly updating them with new information. Additionally, chatbots need to be able to understand the context and nuances of a conversation, which can be particularly challenging in the case of language learning where the chatbot needs to understand the grammar, syntax, and vocabulary of the target language.

Another concern is the potential for the technology to reinforce biases or stereotypes that are present in the training data. For example, if the ChatGPT model is trained on a dataset that contains gender or racial biases, it may inadvertently perpetuate these biases in its responses to users. As such, it is important for developers and educators to carefully consider the training data that is used to train ChatGPT models, and to take steps to mitigate any biases or distortions that may be present.

Another challenge is ensuring that ChatGPT-powered applications are accessible to all students, including those with disabilities or who are from non-English speaking backgrounds. This requires designing applications that are easy to use and navigate, and that can accommodate different learning styles and abilities. It also requires ensuring that the language used by

Another challenge is the need for ChatGPT models to be continuously updated and improved over time. This is particularly important in the field of education, where curricula and pedagogical approaches are constantly evolving. To ensure that ChatGPT remains an effective tool for educators and students, it is essential to stay up-to-date with the latest developments in the field of natural language processing and machine learning, and to be willing to adapt and modify ChatGPT models as necessary.

In conclusion, ChatGPT has the potential to be a powerful tool for transforming education, both by providing personalized support and feedback to students, and by serving as a teaching tool in its own right. While there are certainly challenges and risks associated with the use of ChatGPT in education, with careful planning and implementation, it is possible to harness the power of this technology to improve learning outcomes and enhance the educational experience for students of all ages and backgrounds.

# Chapter 11. ChatGPT for Creative Writing

As the field of natural language processing continues to advance, there are many exciting ways in which AI-powered writing tools like ChatGPT can be applied to enhance creative writing. With its ability to generate natural language text that can mimic the writing style and tone of different authors, ChatGPT is a powerful tool that can be used to aid in the writing process, whether that be through generating ideas, alternate phrasing, character development, or even helping to generate entire stories.

## Using ChatGPT for Creative Writing

One of the most obvious ways in which ChatGPT can be used for creative writing is by generating ideas. By inputting a prompt or topic into the model, ChatGPT can generate a wide range of ideas that can be used as inspiration for further writing. For example, if a writer is stuck on a particular scene in a story, they can input a brief description of the scene and allow ChatGPT to generate several different directions the scene could take. These ideas can be generated based on a wide range of parameters, including genre, style, tone, and even specific keywords. By using ChatGPT to generate ideas, writers can free up their creative energy to focus on the actual writing, rather than getting bogged down in the ideation process.

In addition to generating ideas, ChatGPT can also be used to suggest alternative phrasing. When writing, it can be easy to get stuck in a rut, using the same words and sentence structures repeatedly. ChatGPT can suggest alternative ways of phrasing a sentence, which can help to keep the writing fresh and engaging. This can be particularly useful in creative writing, where the writer is trying to create a unique and compelling voice for their work.

Another way in which ChatGPT can aid in the writing process is by providing inspiration for character development. ChatGPT can be used to generate character profiles, which can include details such as physical appearance, personality traits, and even backstories. By using ChatGPT to generate these profiles, writers can gain new insights and ideas about their characters, which can help to enhance the believability and depth of their writing.

Perhaps one of the most exciting ways in which ChatGPT can be used in creative writing is through its ability to generate entire stories. While this is certainly not a replacement for human creativity, it can be a useful tool for generating first drafts or for getting past writer's block. By inputting a prompt or topic, ChatGPT can generate a short story or even a longer work of fiction. These generated works can then be used as a starting point for further writing, or they can be edited and revised to create a final product.

While the use of AI-powered writing tools like ChatGPT in creative writing is a relatively new field, there are already many examples of successful applications. One such example is the use of AI-generated stories in the field of children's literature.

By providing the model with specific details about the age range and interests of the target audience, AI-generated stories can be created that are tailored specifically to that audience. This can help to increase engagement and interest in reading among children, while also providing a valuable tool for educators and parents.

Another example of the use of ChatGPT in creative writing is in the field of screenwriting. By using ChatGPT to generate ideas for plot points and dialogue, screenwriters can save time and increase the efficiency of the writing process. This can be especially helpful in the fast-paced world of television, where writers are often working under tight deadlines.

## Challenges of Using ChatGPT for Creative Writing

As with any new technology, there are some concerns about the use of ChatGPT in creative writing. One concern is that the use of AI-generated content may lead to a loss of creativity and originality in the writing process. However, proponents of AI-powered writing tools argue that they can be used to enhance, rather than replace, the creative process. By providing writers with new ideas and insights, ChatGPT can help to stimulate creativity and enhance the quality of the writing.

Another challenge is ensuring that the generated content is original and not simply a rehash of existing works. Plagiarism is a serious issue in creative writing, and using a tool like ChatGPT to generate content can increase the risk of unintentional plagiarism. Therefore, it is important to carefully review and edit any content generated by ChatGPT to ensure that it is original and not plagiarized.

Another challenge is ensuring that the content generated by ChatGPT is appropriate for the intended audience. The model is trained on a large corpus of text, much of which may not be appropriate for all audiences. For example, if the intended audience is children, it is important to ensure that the content generated by ChatGPT is suitable for that age group. This may require additional filtering or monitoring of the output generated by the model.

Finally, it is important to recognize the limitations of ChatGPT when using it for creative writing. While the model is capable of generating a wide range of responses, it is not capable of understanding context or nuance in the same way that a human writer can. Therefore, it is important to use ChatGPT as a tool to augment human creativity, rather than as a replacement for it.

# Part V: Ethics, Limitations, and the Future of ChatGPT

## Chapter 12. Ethical Considerations for ChatGPT

ChatGPT and other AI models have become increasingly sophisticated and powerful in recent years, with the potential to revolutionize the way we live and work. However, as with any powerful technology, there are ethical considerations that must be taken into account when using ChatGPT.

One of the primary ethical concerns with ChatGPT is its potential for misuse. As we have seen with other AI models, there is always a risk that ChatGPT could be used for nefarious purposes, such as spreading disinformation, manipulating public opinion, or even committing crimes. This risk is particularly acute given ChatGPT's ability to generate highly convincing text that is difficult to distinguish from human-written content. To mitigate this risk, it is important for developers and users of ChatGPT to implement safeguards and best practices that promote responsible use of the technology. One such safeguard is the use of robust ethical guidelines that outline the acceptable uses of ChatGPT and establish clear boundaries for what is and is not permissible. These guidelines should be developed in consultation with relevant stakeholders, including experts in AI ethics, legal professionals, and civil society groups.

Another important ethical consideration is the potential for ChatGPT to perpetuate bias and discrimination. Like any machine learning model, ChatGPT is only as good as the data it is trained on. If the data used to train ChatGPT is biased or discriminatory in nature, this can lead to the model producing biased or discriminatory results. To address this concern, it is important to ensure that the data used to train ChatGPT is diverse, inclusive, and free from bias. This may require collecting new data that more accurately reflects the diversity of human experience, as well as implementing techniques such as data augmentation to increase the diversity of existing datasets. In addition to ensuring that the data used to train ChatGPT is inclusive and unbiased, it is also important to monitor the model's performance over time to ensure that it is not perpetuating bias or discrimination in its output. This may require ongoing testing and evaluation of the model's performance, as well as the use of techniques such as counterfactual analysis to identify and address biases in the model.

A related ethical concern with ChatGPT is its potential for misuse in the creation of fake or misleading content. As we have seen with deepfakes and other AI-generated content, there is a risk that ChatGPT could be used to create highly convincing fake text that is indistinguishable from genuine content. This could have serious implications for public trust and could even be used to spread disinformation or commit fraud. To address this concern, it is important to implement safeguards that help users identify and distinguish between genuine and fake content. This may include the use of digital watermarks or other forms of metadata that help identify the source of the content, as well as the use of fact-checking and verification tools to help users evaluate the authenticity of the content.

Another important ethical consideration with ChatGPT is the potential for the technology to exacerbate existing inequalities and power imbalances. If ChatGPT is primarily used by a small, privileged group of individuals or organizations, this could lead to further marginalization and exclusion of already underrepresented groups. To address this concern, it is important to ensure that ChatGPT is accessible and affordable to a wide range of users, including those from underrepresented and marginalized communities. This may require the development of new training programs and educational resources that help ensure that these communities have the skills and resources needed to effectively use the technology.

There are also broader ethical considerations related to the use of AI and machine learning more generally. For example, there are concerns about the impact of AI on employment, privacy, and the distribution of power in society. As such, it is important for organizations and individuals using ChatGPT to engage in broader discussions about the ethical implications of AI and machine learning.

Finally, it is important to ensure that the use of ChatGPT is aligned with broader social and ethical values. This may require engaging in public dialogue and consultation with stakeholders to ensure that the use of the technology reflects the values and priorities of society as a whole. This may also require the development of new regulatory frameworks to address the ethical, legal, and social implications of using conversational AI. For example, there may be concerns around data privacy, algorithmic bias, and the potential impact of AI on employment and human agency. To address these issues, it may be necessary to establish guidelines and codes of conduct for the use of ChatGPT, as well as mechanisms for oversight and accountability. By taking a proactive and transparent approach to the ethical and social dimensions of ChatGPT, it is possible to ensure that this powerful technology is used in ways that benefit all members of society.

# Chapter 13. Limitations and Challenges of ChatGPT

Despite the many potential benefits of ChatGPT, there are several key limitations and challenges that must be considered when using and developing the technology. Understanding these limitations and challenges is critical for anyone who is considering using ChatGPT, whether for research, business, or other purposes. Some of the most significant issues include the following:

## Computational Requirements

One of the biggest challenges with ChatGPT is its computational requirements. ChatGPT is a very large model, with billions of parameters, and training it from scratch requires an enormous amount of computational power. Even fine-tuning an existing pre-trained model can be computationally intensive, especially if you are working with a large dataset. This can be a significant obstacle for researchers and businesses that do not have access to large computing clusters or cloud computing resources.

## Complexity of Model Development

Closely related to the limitation of computational requirements is the complexity of model development. While the pre-trained models that underpin ChatGPT are highly sophisticated, developing custom models can be a complex and time-consuming process. This requires a deep understanding of natural language processing and machine learning principles, as well as access to large amounts of high-quality training data. For many organizations, this level of expertise and resources may be out of reach.

## Limited Understanding of Context and Causal Relationships

While ChatGPT is highly adept at generating responses to specific prompts and questions, it is limited in its ability to fully understand and contextualize the conversations it is engaged in. This can lead to responses that are accurate but lack nuance or an appropriate level of emotional intelligence. In other words, ChatGPT may not always be able to "read between the lines" or pick up on subtle cues that a human conversational partner would easily recognize.

Relatedly, ChatGPT is unable to reason about causal relationships. While ChatGPT can generate highly contextually appropriate responses based on the input it receives, it does not have the ability to reason about cause and effect. This means that it is not capable of making inferences or drawing conclusions based on the information it has received. This can be a significant limitation in certain applications, such as medical diagnosis or legal decision-making, where causal relationships are critical.

## Accuracy and Quality of Responses

Due to this limited understanding of context, another challenge is the quality of the generated text.

While ChatGPT is capable of producing highly coherent and contextually appropriate responses, it is not perfect. In some cases, the generated text may be nonsensical, inappropriate, or even offensive. This is a significant concern, particularly when it comes to applications such as customer service or education, where the quality of the responses can have a significant impact on the user experience. It is important to carefully monitor and evaluate the performance of ChatGPT in these contexts, and to have human moderators available to intervene when necessary.

## Potential for Bias and Stereotyping

Like all AI models, ChatGPT is only as unbiased as the data that is used to train it. If the training data is biased or skewed in some way, this can lead to the perpetuation of negative stereotypes or other problematic patterns of thinking in the generated text. This is especially concerning when ChatGPT is used in situations where it is expected to interact with a diverse range of users or in contexts where sensitive or contentious issues are being discussed. For example, if the training data is biased against a particular demographic group, ChatGPT may be more likely to generate responses that are biased against that group. It is critical to carefully evaluate the training data used to train ChatGPT and to take steps to address any potential biases.

## Privacy and Security Concerns

As with any NLP tool that uses large amounts of data, there is always the risk of sensitive information being leaked, misused, or stolen. This is particularly true in the case of ChatGPT, which requires access to large amounts of text data to train and generate responses. This is especially problematic given the highly sensitive nature of many of the conversations that ChatGPT is involved in, including those related to personal or financial information. Ensuring the security of these conversations is critical to maintaining user trust and avoiding potentially serious legal and reputational consequences. It is critical to implement appropriate data security and privacy measures, such as data anonymization and access controls, to protect against these risks.

## Scalability and Overreliance

While the scalability of ChatGPT is one of its strengths, the rapid expansion of its use can also create problems. As more organizations adopt the technology, there is a risk of ChatGPT becoming overburdened and unable to handle the volume of requests it receives. This can lead to slow response times, increased errors, and a decline in overall performance.

Similarly, another challenge involves the potential for overreliance on these models in certain applications. While chatbots and other NLP applications can be incredibly useful and efficient tools, they should never replace human interaction entirely. In some cases, it may be more appropriate or effective to use a human expert or specialist instead of relying solely on a chatbot or NLP model.

## Ethical Concerns

As discussed extensively in the previous chapter, ChatGPT raises a host of ethical considerations, ranging from concerns about privacy and data ownership to broader questions about the impact of AI on society as a whole. For example, some have argued that the use of ChatGPT in customer service contexts could contribute to the erosion of meaningful human relationships and a further depersonalization of society. Similarly, the use of ChatGPT in creative writing contexts raises questions about the authenticity of creative expression and the potential for intellectual property disputes.

## Lack of Transparency

While many of the pre-trained models used by ChatGPT are open-source and freely available, there is often a lack of transparency about how these models were developed and what data was used to train them. This can make it difficult to fully evaluate the quality and potential biases of the models, and may limit the ability of researchers and other stakeholders to build on or improve the technology.

## Early Adoption

Finally, it is worth noting that the field of NLP is still in its early stages, and there is much to be learned and discovered in the years to come. While models like ChatGPT represent a significant advancement in the field, there are still many unanswered questions and challenges that need to be addressed in order to fully realize the potential of NLP technology. As such, it is important for researchers, developers, and other stakeholders to continue exploring and pushing the boundaries of what is possible with NLP, while also remaining mindful of the limitations and challenges associated with this technology.

Despite these challenges, ChatGPT is a powerful and exciting NLP tool that has the potential to revolutionize a wide range of applications, from customer service to education to creative writing. However, it is important to understand the limitations and challenges associated with this tool, including its computational requirements, the quality of the generated text, privacy and security concerns, its inability to reason about causal relationships, and the risk of bias in the generated text. By carefully considering these factors and implementing appropriate safeguards, it is possible to use ChatGPT in a responsible and effective manner that benefits both users and businesses.

# Chapter 14. Future of ChatGPT and NLP

The field of natural language processing (NLP) is constantly evolving and improving, and ChatGPT is no exception. As researchers and developers continue to work on improving NLP technology, there are several exciting trends and developments on the horizon for ChatGPT. ChatGPT has made significant strides in the field of natural language processing, and its future looks bright as it continues to evolve. The technology is being used across a variety of industries, and there is no doubt that it will continue to have a significant impact on how we communicate with machines in the future. In this chapter, we will delve deeper into some of the key trends and emerging technologies in NLP and examine their potential impact on society.

One of the most significant trends in NLP is the growing use of deep learning algorithms and neural networks, which have revolutionized the field by enabling machines to learn from vast amounts of data and make increasingly accurate predictions about language use and meaning. These technologies have been instrumental in enabling applications such as speech recognition and machine translation, and they are also driving new innovations in areas such as sentiment analysis, chatbots, and document summarization.

However, as these technologies become more advanced and powerful, there is a growing concern about their potential impact on the labor market, as many routine tasks that were once performed by humans are now being automated. This is particularly true in the area of customer service, where chatbots and virtual assistants are increasingly being used to handle routine inquiries and requests. While these technologies have the potential to increase efficiency and reduce costs, they may also lead to job displacement and exacerbate existing inequalities in the labor market.

Another emerging trend in NLP is the use of natural language understanding (NLU) technologies, which enable machines to interpret and respond to human language in a more sophisticated and nuanced way. This is particularly important in applications such as virtual assistants and chatbots, where the ability to understand and respond to complex queries and requests is critical. NLU technologies are also driving new innovations in areas such as sentiment analysis and opinion mining, which can help organizations better understand customer preferences and feedback.

However, there are also concerns about the potential for bias and unfairness in NLU technologies, particularly with respect to their ability to understand and respond to diverse dialects, accents, and speech patterns. There is also a risk that these technologies may reinforce existing biases and stereotypes, particularly if they are trained on biased or limited data sets. To address these concerns, researchers and developers in the field of NLP are working to develop more inclusive and diverse training data sets, as well as more transparent and accountable algorithms that can be audited and evaluated for fairness and accuracy.

Another key area of focus for ChatGPT development is the continued refinement of its language generation capabilities. As more data is fed into the system and as machine learning algorithms continue to improve, ChatGPT will be able to generate more complex and nuanced responses to user input. This will make ChatGPT an even more powerful tool for a variety of applications, from customer service to creative writing. Additionally, ChatGPT is improving its ability to understand and respond to human emotions. Emotion detection is a key area of research in the field of NLP, and as this technology continues to improve, it will enable ChatGPT to tailor its responses to better meet the emotional needs of its users. This could have significant implications for a variety of applications, from mental health chatbots to marketing and customer service.

These chatbots can simulate conversations with human users, and are increasingly being used in customer service and other applications where human-like interaction is required. With its advanced natural language processing capabilities, ChatGPT can provide highly accurate and natural-sounding responses to user input. Chatbots are typically trained on large amounts of conversational data, which allows them to learn the patterns and structures of human language. ChatGPT is particularly well-suited for this task, as it can generate responses that are indistinguishable from those of a human user. This makes it an ideal tool for creating chatbots that can provide high-quality customer service and support, without the need for human intervention.

Another area of emerging innovation in NLP is the use of generative models, which enable machines to create new language and generate text that is highly realistic and convincing. This technology has significant potential for applications such as creative writing, content generation, and even news reporting. However, it also presents significant ethical and social challenges, particularly with respect to the potential for fake news and misinformation.

As these technologies become more advanced and accessible, it is essential for society to have a broader conversation about their implications and potential impact. This includes considering questions such as: what are the ethical considerations associated with the use of generative models in various domains, such as journalism or politics? How can we ensure that these technologies are developed and used in a way that promotes transparency, accountability, and trust? And what are the potential risks and negative impacts of these technologies, and how can we mitigate them?

In addition to these specific trends and emerging technologies, there are also broader societal and cultural shifts that are likely to shape the future of NLP. For example, as the world becomes more globalized and interconnected, there is a growing need for NLP technologies that can facilitate communication and understanding across different languages and cultures. There is also a growing interest in NLP applications that can support education and learning, such as intelligent tutoring systems and personalized language learning platforms.

Furthermore, as NLP technologies become more ubiquitous and powerful, there is a growing need for researchers and developers to engage in a more open and transparent dialogue with stakeholders and end-users. This includes sharing information about the development and deployment of NLP models, as well as being transparent about the potential limitations and biases that may be present in these models.

There is a growing awareness of the ethical implications of NLP technologies, and many organizations are working to ensure that these technologies are developed and used in a responsible and ethical manner. For example, the Partnership on AI is a coalition of companies, researchers, and advocacy organizations that are working to develop and promote responsible AI technologies. The group has developed a set of guidelines for the development and deployment of AI systems, including NLP models, that prioritize ethical considerations such as transparency, accountability, and fairness.

Another important application of ChatGPT is in language translation and multilingual support. Currently, ChatGPT is primarily trained on English-language data, which limits its usefulness in multilingual contexts. However, there is a growing need for NLP tools that can handle multiple languages, and as a result, there is a significant amount of research focused on improving the multilingual capabilities of NLP systems. However, with ChatGPT's ability to understand the context of a sentence, ChatGPT can translate text from one language to another with a high degree of accuracy. This is achieved by training the model on large amounts of parallel text, which is text that has been translated into multiple languages. By analyzing the patterns and structures of these translations, ChatGPT can learn to accurately translate sentences from one language to another.

Language translation is a highly complex task, as there are often many ways to express the same idea in different languages. Additionally, different languages have different grammatical structures and idiomatic expressions that may not have a direct translation in other languages. However, with its advanced natural language processing capabilities, ChatGPT can take these nuances into account and produce translations that accurately convey the meaning of the original text.

Another use case for ChatGPT is in the field of summarization. With the vast amount of information available on the internet, it can be difficult to sort through and extract the most important points. However, with ChatGPT's ability to understand the context and meaning of text, it can summarize long documents and articles into concise and informative summaries.

This is achieved by training the model on large amounts of text data, and then using it to identify the most important sentences and concepts in a document. The resulting summary is a condensed version of the original text that captures the key points and ideas, allowing users to quickly get a sense of the information without having to read the entire document.

One of the most significant developments in the future of ChatGPT is the ongoing research in developing more powerful and efficient models. Current models have already demonstrated impressive performance on a wide range of natural language tasks, but researchers continue to explore new ways to enhance the underlying algorithms and architectures.

One of the most promising directions for future development is the use of more sophisticated training methods. While supervised learning has been the primary approach to training NLP models, researchers are exploring more advanced techniques, such as unsupervised and semi-supervised learning. These approaches rely on data sources that are not labeled or only partially labeled, making it possible to train models with less human intervention.

Another promising direction for ChatGPT's future is its integration with other technologies, such as computer vision and speech recognition. This integration could enable chatbots and other NLP applications to better understand and interpret a broader range of input data. For example, a chatbot designed to assist with travel planning could use computer vision to analyze photos of a user's travel destination and incorporate that information into its recommendations.

As NLP models like ChatGPT become more complex, they require increasingly powerful hardware to run effectively. Advances in computing technology, such as the development of more powerful GPUs and specialized NLP processors, will be key in enabling the continued development and deployment of NLP systems like ChatGPT.

Additionally, as the field of NLP continues to evolve, there is a growing need for NLP tools to be integrated with other technologies, such as voice assistants and virtual reality systems. This integration will enable ChatGPT to be used in a wider variety of contexts and will help to further improve its capabilities.

Finally, the future of ChatGPT will depend on the ability of researchers and developers to continue pushing the boundaries of what is possible in natural language processing. As the technology continues to evolve and improve, it is likely that we will see new and innovative applications of chatbots and other NLP technologies, from more powerful virtual assistants to new tools for creative writing and content creation.

Overall, the future of ChatGPT looks bright, with continued advancements in language generation, emotion detection, and multilingual support on the horizon. As NLP technology continues to improve, we can expect to see ChatGPT and other NLP tools playing an increasingly important role in a wide variety of applications, from customer service to education and beyond. ChatGPT is a highly advanced natural language processing model that has a wide range of applications in many different fields. Its ability to understand the context and meaning of text makes it a valuable tool for tasks such as language translation, summarization, and chatbot development. As the field of natural language processing continues to evolve, it is likely that ChatGPT and similar models will play an increasingly important role in the development of new applications and technologies that leverage the power of human language.

# Part VI: Appendices

## Appendix 1. Glossary of Terms

Artificial intelligence (AI) - a field of computer science focused on the creation of intelligent machines that can perform tasks that typically require human-like intelligence, such as visual perception, speech recognition, decision-making, and language translation.

Attention mechanism: A mechanism in deep learning that enables the model to focus its attention on specific parts of the input.

Backpropagation: An algorithm used for training artificial neural networks that adjusts the weights of the network's connections based on the error between the predicted output and the actual output.

BERT (Bidirectional Encoder Representations from Transformers): A pre-trained NLP model developed by Google that uses a transformer architecture to process text.

Chatbot - a software application designed to simulate conversation with human users, especially over the internet.

ChatGPT - an open-source, deep learning-based conversational AI model developed by OpenAI.

Conversational AI - a subset of AI that focuses on creating natural, human-like conversations between machines and humans.

Data augmentation: A technique used to increase the size of a dataset by creating new examples based on existing data.

Data preprocessing: The process of cleaning, transforming, and organizing data to prepare it for use in a machine learning model.

Deep learning - a subset of machine learning that uses artificial neural networks with multiple layers to extract high-level features from raw data and make accurate predictions.

Encoder-decoder architecture: A type of neural network architecture commonly used in machine translation and other NLP tasks.

Fine-tuning - the process of training a pre-existing deep learning model on a new dataset by updating its weights through backpropagation, with the goal of improving its performance on a specific task.

Generative model: A type of model that generates new data, such as images or text, based on a given input.

Generative Pre-training Transformer (GPT): A deep learning model for natural language processing developed by OpenAI, consisting of a multi-layer transformer-based architecture trained on large amounts of text data.

Gradient descent: An optimization algorithm used in machine learning to find the minimum of a loss function.

Language Model: An AI model that is trained to predict the likelihood of a sequence of words or characters based on the context of the surrounding text.

Machine Learning: A field of AI that focuses on the development of algorithms and models that can learn from and make predictions on data without being explicitly programmed.

Natural language generation (NLG): A subfield of NLP that involves generating natural-sounding text.

Natural Language Processing (NLP) - a field of AI focused on the interaction between computers and human language, including tasks such as text classification, sentiment analysis, language translation, and speech recognition.

Natural language understanding (NLU): A subfield of NLP that involves understanding the meaning of human language.

Neural network: A type of machine learning model that is inspired by the structure and function of the human brain.

OpenAI - an artificial intelligence research laboratory consisting of the for-profit company OpenAI LP and its parent company, the non-profit OpenAI Inc.

Overfitting: A phenomenon in machine learning where a model becomes too specialized to the training data and performs poorly on new, unseen data.

Pre-processing: The process of cleaning, normalizing, and transforming raw data to make it suitable for analysis by an AI model.

Pre-training: The process of training a model on a large amount of data to learn general representations that can be applied to specific tasks.

Pre-trained model - a deep learning model that has already been trained on a large dataset, often with the goal of generalizing to new data and tasks.

Recurrent Neural Network (RNN): A type of artificial neural network designed to process sequential data by using feedback loops to pass information between network layers.

Scaling - the process of increasing the capacity and performance of a deep learning model by distributing the training process across multiple computing devices or clusters.

Sentiment Analysis: A type of NLP that involves analyzing the emotion, tone, and polarity of text data, often used for measuring customer satisfaction or predicting public opinion.

Sequence-to-sequence (seq2seq) - a type of deep learning model that is designed to map sequences of input data to sequences of output data.

Tokenization: The process of breaking up a sentence or document into individual words or tokens, which can be used as inputs to an AI model.

Transformer architecture - a type of deep learning architecture that uses self-attention mechanisms to model dependencies between input and output sequences.

Transfer Learning: A machine learning technique that involves using a pre-trained model to solve a new problem with limited labeled data, often through fine-tuning a pre-trained model on a new task or dataset.

Underfitting: A phenomenon in machine learning where a model is too simple to capture the complexity of the data, leading to poor performance on both training and test data.

Unsupervised learning - a type of machine learning where the model is trained on data without explicit supervision, often with the goal of discovering hidden patterns or structure in the data.

Virtual assistant - an AI-based system that is designed to provide assistance or perform tasks for humans, often through natural language interactions.

Word Embedding: A technique for representing words in a numerical format that preserves the semantic relationships between them, often used as input features for NLP models.

Zero-shot learning: A type of machine learning in which a model can make predictions on tasks it has not been explicitly trained on.

# Appendix 2. Additional Resources

If you're interested in learning more about ChatGPT, natural language processing, and deep learning, here are some resources you might find useful:

## Online Courses and Tutorials

- Practical Deep Learning for Coders: A free, online course that covers deep learning with a focus on practical applications. The course is taught using the PyTorch framework, which is used in ChatGPT. (https://course.fast.ai/)

- Natural Language Processing with Deep Learning in Python: A comprehensive course on NLP and deep learning, covering topics such as sentiment analysis, machine translation, and chatbots. (https://www.udemy.com/course/natural-language-processing-with-deep-learning-in-python/)

- TensorFlow Tutorial for Beginners: A collection of tutorials that cover the basics of the TensorFlow framework, which is another popular deep learning framework. (https://www.tensorflow.org/tutorials)

## Books

- Deep Learning with Python: A book by François Chollet, the creator of the Keras deep learning framework. The book covers deep learning concepts and practical applications in

Python, and includes several example projects. (https://www.manning.com/books/deep-learning-with-python)

- Speech and Language Processing: A textbook by Dan Jurafsky and James H. Martin that provides an introduction to NLP and covers topics such as syntax, semantics, and machine translation. (https://web.stanford.edu/~jurafsky/slp3/)

- The Hundred-Page Machine Learning Book: A book by Andriy Burkov that provides a concise introduction to machine learning concepts and algorithms, with a focus on practical applications. (https://leanpub.com/theMLbook)

## Open Source Software

- Hugging Face: A platform that provides access to pre-trained NLP models, including ChatGPT, and tools for fine-tuning and deploying these models. (https://huggingface.co/)

- PyTorch: An open source deep learning framework that is used in ChatGPT and many other deep learning applications. (https://pytorch.org/)

- TensorFlow: Another popular open source deep learning framework that is used in many applications, including NLP. (https://www.tensorflow.org/)

## Research Papers

- Attention Is All You Need: A paper by Ashish Vaswani et al. that introduced the Transformer architecture, which is used in ChatGPT and many other NLP models. (https://arxiv.org/abs/1706.03762)

- BERT: Pre-training of Deep Bidirectional Transformers for Language Understanding: A paper by Jacob Devlin et al. that introduced the BERT model, which is another popular pre-trained NLP model. (https://arxiv.org/abs/1810.04805)

- GPT-2: Language Models Are Unsupervised Multitask Learners: A paper by Alec Radford et al. that introduced the GPT-2 model, which is a larger and more powerful version of ChatGPT. (https://d4mucfpksywv.cloudfront.net/better-language-models/language-models.pdf)

These resources provide a good starting point for learning more about ChatGPT, NLP, and deep learning. With the growing importance of language-based applications and the increasing capabilities of NLP technologies, this field is likely to see many more exciting developments in the years to come.

# Appendix 3. ChatGPT FAQ

Below are some of the most commonly-asked questions regarding ChatGPT. Throughout this book, we have tried to answer these questions in exacting detail, but for those that need a quick answer, now: we offer the following FAQ.

Q: What is ChatGPT?

A: ChatGPT is an artificial intelligence language model developed by OpenAI that uses deep learning to generate text-based conversations with humans.

Q: How does ChatGPT work?

A: ChatGPT is a generative model that has been trained on a large corpus of text data to predict the next word in a sequence of words. It uses a deep learning algorithm called a transformer to analyze the input text and generate output text based on that analysis.

Q: Can I use ChatGPT for my own chatbot?

A: Yes, you can use ChatGPT as the core of your chatbot, and you can fine-tune it on your own data to make it more specific to your use case.

Q: How accurate is ChatGPT?

A: The accuracy of ChatGPT depends on the quality and quantity of the training data used to train the model. In general, it can generate high-quality responses, but it may also produce inaccurate or irrelevant responses in some cases.

Q: How do I fine-tune ChatGPT for my specific use case?

A: To fine-tune ChatGPT, you need to have a dataset of conversations or other text data that is relevant to your use case. You can use the Hugging Face Transformers library to fine-tune the pre-trained model on your own data.

Q: What are some best practices for using ChatGPT?

A: Some best practices for using ChatGPT include training the model on a high-quality dataset, validating the responses to ensure accuracy and relevance, monitoring the performance of the chatbot over time, and being transparent with users about the use of AI in the chatbot.

Q: Is ChatGPT biased?

A: Like all machine learning models, ChatGPT can be biased if the training data contains biased language or reflects biased societal views. It is important to carefully select and preprocess the training data to reduce bias.

Q: What are some limitations of ChatGPT?

A: Some limitations of ChatGPT include the potential for generating inaccurate or irrelevant responses, the inability to understand the context of the conversation, and the risk of perpetuating bias in the training data.

Q: What are some potential use cases for ChatGPT?

A: ChatGPT can be used for a wide range of applications, including customer service chatbots, personal assistants, language translation, creative writing, and more.

Q: Is ChatGPT the best chatbot solution?

A: ChatGPT is one of the most powerful and flexible chatbot solutions available, but there is no one "best" solution for all use cases. The best chatbot solution depends on the specific needs and requirements of your use case.

Q: Can ChatGPT be used to generate fake news or manipulate public opinion?

A: Unfortunately, there is a risk that AI-generated content like that produced by ChatGPT could be used to spread misinformation or propaganda. It's important to use the technology responsibly and to have systems in place to verify the accuracy of information generated by the model.

Q: Is ChatGPT open source?

A: Yes, the original GPT model was developed by OpenAI and released as an open-source project. However, some of the more recent versions of GPT, including GPT-2 and GPT-3, are not open source and require a license to use.

Q: What are some potential applications of ChatGPT beyond chatbots?

A: While chatbots are one of the most popular applications of ChatGPT, the technology has many other potential uses. For example, it could be used to generate product descriptions, answer customer service inquiries, or provide personalized recommendations to users.

Q: Can ChatGPT understand multiple languages?

A: While the original GPT model was trained on English text, there are efforts to train models on other languages as well. However, this is still an active area of research and development, and currently most

ChatGPT models are designed to work with English text.

Q: What hardware is required to run a ChatGPT model?

A: Running a ChatGPT model requires significant computing power, and most applications will require specialized hardware such as a graphics processing unit (GPU) or a tensor processing unit (TPU). Cloud-based services like AWS, Azure, and Google Cloud offer the ability to rent these types of resources on a pay-per-use basis.

Q: What is the difference between fine-tuning and training a ChatGPT model?

A: Fine-tuning involves taking a pre-trained ChatGPT model and retraining it on a specific task or dataset. This allows the model to adapt to the specific requirements of the task at hand. Training a model from scratch, on the other hand, involves initializing the model's weights randomly and training it on a large dataset from the ground up.

Q: How can I get started with ChatGPT if I'm a beginner?

A: There are many online resources available for beginners who want to learn more about ChatGPT and NLP. Some popular resources include the OpenAI

API, Hugging Face's Transformers library, and the Fast.ai course on practical deep learning for coders. Additionally, there are many tutorials and example projects available on GitHub and other code-sharing platforms.

Q: Can ChatGPT be used for languages other than English?

A: Yes, ChatGPT can be fine-tuned on data in other languages, although the quality of the responses may vary depending on the amount and quality of the training data. Additionally, there are pre-trained GPT models available for some other languages besides English.

Q: How does ChatGPT compare to other chatbot frameworks like Dialogflow or Microsoft Bot Framework?

A: ChatGPT is different from these frameworks in that it is specifically designed for generating human-like responses in natural language. Dialogflow and Bot Framework are more general-purpose platforms that can be used for building chatbots with specific functionality, such as task-oriented bots that can help with customer service or booking appointments.

Q: Can ChatGPT be used for generating text other than chatbot responses?

A: Yes, ChatGPT can be fine-tuned on data from a variety of sources and used to generate text in other contexts, such as generating product descriptions or even writing news articles. However, it is important to keep in mind that the model is designed to generate text that is similar to the training data, so it may not be suitable for all applications.

Q: What are the hardware requirements for training and running ChatGPT models?

A: Training a large ChatGPT model can be computationally expensive and may require specialized hardware such as graphics processing units (GPUs) or tensor processing units (TPUs). Running a pre-trained ChatGPT model for inference can be done on a standard CPU, although faster hardware may provide improved performance.

Q: How does ChatGPT handle sensitive or personal information?

A: ChatGPT is a machine learning model that is only as good as the training data it has been exposed to, so it is important to be mindful of the privacy implications of using the model with sensitive information. If used in a context where personal information is being exchanged, it may be necessary to build in additional safeguards to protect the privacy and security of the users. Additionally, it is important to be transparent with users about how their data is being used and who has access to it.